FROM DESTRUCTION

2

A REDEEMED WOMAN

*Woman Marked 4 Death & Destruction
That Finds Redemption In Christ*

PALMETTO
PUBLISHING
Charleston, SC
www.PalmettoPublishing.com

Hardcover ISBN: 979-8-8229-4268-4
Paperback ISBN: 979-8-8229-4269-1
eBook ISBN: 979-8-8229-4270-7

YOLANDA BEASLEY

FROM DESTRUCTION

2

A REDEEMED WOMAN

*Woman Marked 4 Death & Destruction
That Finds Redemption In Christ*

Contents

Dedication

This book is dedicated to all the girls, women, boys, and men who have had tragic beginnings and have found themselves still trying to get through life with the memories of past pain. Christ is a redeemer; I'm a living witness that tragedy and its stain doesn't have to be your final end.

I would like to first thank and give glory and all reverence to Christ who is my Lord and Savior and who has made every breath I take possible. Like the apostle Paul said in Ephesians 3:1, I am a "prisoner of Christ Jesus" (KJV). I am truly a prisoner of Christ by choice and by His unmatched and unimaginable favor, mercy, and grace.

I would like to thank my grandmother Stella Beasley for setting the foundation of Christ for this troubled family and my mom, Linda Beasley, for continuing to laying the foundation, for passing the torch of God, for praying many nights, and for being part of the village that helped raise my kids.

I would like to thank my dad, James David Carter, who will never know the impact he had on me in the short time that he lived. The love and adoration I had for him as a little girl meant I didn't care where he was as long as I was there. I appreciate the love he gave to me and showed as a daddy.

I would like to thank my kids—all six of them—for teaching me the good, the bad, and the ugly of parenting. I thank my grandchildren who give me grandma joy.

Finally, I'd like to thank attorney Earl Jackson. There are no words I can say to describe how grateful I am for all his years of running to the courthouse and accepting many collect phone calls from jail. Thank you for giving me hard words when I needed to hear them; thank you for everything. I know God predestined you to be in my life.

And thank you to all my family who had both a positive and negative impact on my life. To all my loved ones, thank you; I love you all.

Chapter 1: Daddy's Little Girl

I remember running to the window and looking out to see if my daddy had pulled up. I had to be five or six years old, and I was waiting for him to come pick up me, my sister Tonya, and my cousin Jackie for the week (or however long he was going to keep us). Waiting for my dad always felt like waiting for Santa Claus. I so loved this man, and not just because I always knew we were getting something new. I just loved being with my dad no matter where he was—which wasn't always the best of places to take children. After leaving the military, my dad was the epitome of a '70s hustler, and this was the '70s. I used to love looking at him and playing with his hair; he literally looked just like Ron O'Neal from *Super Fly* (and I thought he was). I loved being with him even when he had us in the gambling house; I didn't care, I just wanted to be with him because I always felt protected and I knew I was protected. My dad had gambling and drug spots in Dallas, Texas. My dad had four children by three different women, and no matter what, he managed to keep his kids with him or around him. I had a stepbrother (though we didn't get to see him often because his mom wasn't always ok with me and my sister Tonya) and another stepsister who was older.

I saw his car pull up, ran to the door, opened it, and grabbed him as if it would take pliers to pry us apart. He hugged me and kissed me and, as always, called me and Tonya his favorite words: "Hey, fleabag and catfish!" I didn't care what it meant, I was just happy to see him. We all left: me, Tonya, and Jackie. He always took Jackie along with us; she was our big sister and was the boss of us. Jackie was three years older than me and did our hair and fed us but mainly kept me out of trouble. (Yep, I was the defiant one and had do everything I wasn't supposed to and got everyone in trouble.) I remember pulling up at my grandpa and his wife's home; we had arrived in Fairfield in the country. My grandpa had a farm, and I didn't like going because we would have to get up early to go load his truck and feed swains. But not this trip. He ended up taking us down the road to what look like a ole country store with an attached building. We went in and ordered burgers, and he took us upstairs to what seemed to be an unfinished apartment being renovated. We stayed there for about two weeks, which meant he was there on business.

Chapter 2: California Road Trip

There was a knock on the door; it had to be after 1:00 a.m. We were staying the night at my aunt Minnie's who was one of my dad's best friends and my mom's oldest sister. It was my dad at the door. He walked in, and we were asleep on the floor with the rest of cousins. He came to me, tapped me on the shoulder, and said, "Wake up, fleabag, we going on a trip." Then he woke everyone and shouted, "Whoever wants to go, get up, don't pack anything, let's go." I remember it being me, my sister Tonya, my mom, my aunt Bobby (my mom's baby sister), Bobby's daughter (my other sister cousin) Chandra, my cousin Maurice, and my cousin Sharon (who was nine months pregnant). We loaded up in this traveling van that looked like small mobile home; it had a toilet and was big enough for everyone. I remember stopping, Daddy buying what we needed, and then off we went on a road trip to California—what would be a long road vacation and the last trip we would make with my daddy. We stopped at the Grand Canyon and took pictures in tepees. It was amazing. I was on cloud nine because I was with my dad, the only person I thought loved me, and I loved him. We arrived in California, we enjoyed ourselves, and then back to Dallas we went.

Years later, I was told that Daddy wasn't only there for a family trip; it was supposed to be a last business deal. My daddy was a professional gambler and sold drugs.

Chapter 3: My First Heartbreak

After coming back to Dallas, it was state fair time. We came back to Dallas on October 18th, and the state fair was on the 19th. We were waiting on my dad to pick us up from my aunt Minnie's house to take us to the fair. I was playing with my barbie doll and van, and my aunt came in the room and said, "Call your dad to see when he is picking y'all up." I'm not sure where my mom was. At the age of eight, I knew two phone numbers: one was the number to the main gambling house in Oak Cliff and the other was. I called the number, and an unknown man (whose voice sounded like a white man's) answered and said, "James Carter is out of business." Then he hung up the phone. I didn't think anything of it and returned to playing.

My aunt came back in about thirty minutes later and asked, "Did you call your dad?"

I answered, "Yes, but a white man picked up and said 'James Carter is out of business.'" My aunt told me, "Call again to see what time your dad is picking y'all up."

For the second time I called, and for the second time the same man answered the phone and said, "James Carter is out of business." This time, I also heard arguing and shooting in the background, so I hung up the phone. When my aunt entered the room again, she started fussing at me that I hadn't done what she had asked. I told her they were shooting over there, and the look on her face was a look of fright and disbelief.

My mom and my aunt somehow went back and forth, and by the time everyone had gathered themselves, my mom received a call that my dad was DOA.

I remember his funeral looking like something out of a movie. It was packed, and I remember seeing people who looked like gangsters, hustlers, pimps, etc. from all over. It still didn't hit me that I would never again see the man I loved.

As time went on, during every fair season, I would get depressed and defiant.

Years later, my mom started dating and living with a man I used to refer to (in my mind) as the monster. He would abuse her in front of us, and I mean brutalize her. I used to pray many days that my dad or my uncle John (who was my mom's baby brother) would come help. My uncle John took me under his wing as my protector after the death of my dad. I'm not sure how God worked it, out but she finally left him.

Chapter 4: Growing Pains and Continued Childhood Trauma

The years passed, and I continued to experience moments of tragedy and growing pains. I was molested by two different cousins. I didn't say anything, though, because I was always afraid of my mom beating me. Yes, my mom abused me physically. But I still loved her. However, it was like I reminded her of my dad or something, because I never received the same love from her as she gave to my sister.

My mom married a man who I thought would change our lives, but I was only to get disappointed again. We ended up moving from Oak Cliff to North Dallas, and I was excited. My mom was working at night sometimes, and I started sneaking out of the house. Everyone would meet up at the swimming pool and hang out, listening to music and break dancing. Then I would unlock the front door to sneak back in the house.

Well, I finally got caught sneaking back in one night; my stepdad was sitting in the living room with some items that

I later found out were crack and a pipe. I was twelve years old at this time, and I walked fast toward my bedroom as if I didn't see what was going on. I got in bed with my sister and acted like I was asleep. I started feeling that something bad was about to happen—the same feeling I had when I was molested. I actually thought I was he was going to molest me, but what he did was just as bad and was another form of abuse. My bedroom door opened. I closed my eyes as if I was asleep. My sister Tonya was sound asleep, and I remember getting so close to her so he would have to wake both of us. He stood over me and said, "Potchie, come here; I know you not sleeping." Slowly and with a sick feeling, I got up and walked out of the bedroom toward the living room where he had been sitting when I snuck back in the house. He told me to sit down on the couch and said, "Now, if your mommy find out you been sneaking out, she gonna beat you!"

It was a fact; everyone knew how she abused me. I remember my aunts many times telling her, "Linda, you better stop beating that girl like that." (This was before she got saved; at that point the physical abuse stopped, but other things continued.) I knew I didn't want her to find out, because of how unbearable the beatings were. I won't get into the details of how many times my skin would be open to white tissue. I use to fantasize about running away and getting on a train to wherever it would take me, and at times, I even wanted to die.

My stepdad asked, "What do y'all be doing when y'all be hanging out this late?"

I said, "Nothing, just hanging out."

He asked, "Y'all don't be smoking and drinking?"

I said "No." And that was the truth.

He asked, "Do you know what this is?" He picked up the round chips and glass item. This was the beginning of crack era, so I didn't know what it was. He said, "Here, smoke this and you won't do any drugs when you get older! And if you tell your mama, she gonna beat you for sneaking out."

And so I wouldn't say anything to anyone for years.

Chapter 5: Continued
Growing Pains

It was one of those summers when we had to go to the country. This time it would be to my mom's mother, my grandmother. She lived in Ennis, Texas, and so did my mom's next oldest sister and her husband and their eight kids who were older than all of us. My grandmother would get us up at the crack of dawn, literally before she went to work, and we couldn't stay alone in her house. So we would have to walk down the road to my aunt's, which was ten or fifteen minutes up the road from my granny's. It would still be dark out, and when we could see my aunt's house, we would begin to run the rest of the way, trying to get the only spot left in my aunt's daughter's bed. Whoever didn't would have to sleep on the hardwood floor. My aunt had five boys and one girl, and the boys treated us horribly. They would lock us outside in the heat for hours and wouldn't let us eat or drink water. My aunt had a salon that was connected to the side of the house. My aunt would have lot of clients sitting and getting their hair done. She would be in the shop all day. My uncle was a meek and humble man of God, but he worked as a mail carrier and was a pastor, so he was never there in the day time. So we had no one who would help us. We had to stay there until my granny got off work, which was after 5:00 p.m.

One day we found out God and prayer were real. We were *so* hungry, and our cousins wouldn't let us inside. It was very hot, and we would walk through the fields and up and down the road picking up empty bottles that we could turn in for one cent. Our plan was to pick up enough bottles to get a slice of salami, cheese, crackers, one jungle juice, and two Indian cookies. We were so tired and hot, we had to take a break. There was a huge oak tree that sat off the road not too far from my aunt's home. We all laid out on our backs under the shade, looking up at the sky, and my oldest cousin said, "Let's pray that God will send us some food." We prayed and prayed, and my cousin finally said "Y'all not praying hard enough."

Then God answered our prayers. About an hour later, a car pulled up to the curb by the big tree. The window came down and a voice yelled, "Jackie! Why y'all laying on the ground like that?" We all jumped up at once, looked, and saw it was Jackie's dad. We all jumped in his car and he drove us into town to feed us. I don't remember where we ate, but we got fat and full. And at that point, we knew God was real.

One of my aunt's sons began to molest me during our summer stays there. It was awful. I never said anything; just like the other abuse, I would be grown before I would say anything. I remember us saying, "When we get older, we are never going back to the country." And back to Dallas we went; we were so happy to go back home

Chapter 6: A Child with a Child

I remember having consensual sex at the age of thirteen. I got pregnant with my firstborn, my son Cory David Beasley. I gave him my daddy's middle name, David. Although I was a kid having a kid, I was so excited about having this baby. I didn't know I was pregnant for a long time. I wasn't showing nor having my period until I was almost seven months.

My cousin Jackie came to spend the summer with us. Jackie was in high school at this point. I remember her taking me with her across the street to an abortion clinic because she thought she was pregnant. I never knew it was an abortion clinic, and I never really thought I was pregnant, but they offered free pregnancy tests, so we walked over checked in. We both took a pregnancy test and then sat in the waiting room waiting for the results. Suddenly, the young lady walked out to us, and I was not worried. The lady said, "Well, ladies, you're both positive. Congratulations, you're both having a baby." I fell out of my chair on the floor and was crying.

My cousin was more worried about me than herself. She stood up and said, "Oooooo, your mama is gonna beat you." Everyone knew my mom would literally beat me.

Well, as God would have it, she did not beat me when she found out. But she did say I had to give the baby up for adoption. I spent the next few months not worried, for some reason, about going through with adoption, because I knew I was going to keep this baby. On December 9, 1986, God blessed me with my firstborn son.

Chapter 7: Growing Pains

Every time I got the chance, I ran away. It seemed every time I ran away, I came back home pregnant. Things at home were not getting better. My mom's husband and gotten so bad on crack, and we were going through it and having to move a lot. Through those struggles, God was drawing my mom to Himself, and she got saved.

I somehow managed to stay in school through all the pregnancies and the chaos at home. I made it to my senior year, and of course I was pregnant and working part time in North Park Mall. I was just two and a half months from graduation, and was so excited and proud of myself that I was going to graduate from high school with children.

We were living with my aunt, so me and my sister had to ride the city bus from Oak Cliff to North Dallas to go to school. I remember my mom getting upset because I had just gotten paid. It was always just barely seventy-five dollars. I had to buy Pampers and make sure I had bus fare and lunch money for the next week. And I had given my mom gas money for taking me to pick up my check, so I had but a few bucks left. She demanded that I give my sister some money, and I said no, I didn't have enough money. She got upset and fussed and said since I wouldn't give her any money, I had to stay home from school and keep my own kids. I did not think that she was serious—what parent would punish their child by threatening to keep them from going to school and graduating? So I got up the next morning and started getting dressed for school and my mom got up and said, "I said you not going back to school because I'm not babysitting."

My aunt said, "Sis, Linda, I'll keep the kids while she at school, don't not let her graduate." (We were not only staying with my aunt, but my aunt was a babysitter; she kept kids for a living.)

My mom said to my aunt, "No, I told her last night when she said she wasn't giving Tonya anything that she would have to keep her own kids." Mind you, I had already paid for my cap and gown and senior package. So when she wouldn't let me go back to school, I can't tell you how hurt I was and how I cried. That would be one of many hurts that stiffened my heart toward my mom. One of many growing pains.

After months went by, I was in a car accident and I received a check. I took that money and went put it down on my first apartment. My mom expected me to give her and Tonya some money out of that check, and I said no. I was not over what she had done. She said some horrible things to me and even accused me of being the reason Tonya was now pregnant in her senior year. (I know this sounds unbelievable, especially for a woman in church, but every word is true.) I went and moved with my kids into my first apartment.

Chapter 8: The Biggest Growth Pain and Dysfunction

The apartment I moved into in North Dallas was in the same building where my cousin Jackie lived. I was in a one-bedroom apartment with me and my kids except for my oldest son. He was living with his grandparents—his dad parents. I thank God for them, because they raised him when they didn't have to; they gave him a good life. He would come and visit often. Three or four months later, my sister came to stay with me. She had just graduated from high school and had my nephew Josh, whom I considered my nephewson. He was born with a disease called Chiari malformation type 2, also known as spina bifida, and other health issues. (Later in my adult life, I found that I also had the same disease, but I would be diagnosed with type 1.) Josh would grow to be a blessing to me, and my kids called him their brother. He was a humble and beautiful kid who kept calm when the storm was roaring in my family between my sister, my mom, and my kids.

I was pregnant again during this time, and I had made up in my mind that I would give the baby up. In the state of Texas, they have to contact father and he has to sign as well. This individual didn't know I was pregnant, so he showed up at my place stating he was not going to sign, and he did not. When it was time for me to deliver the baby, *my son* left the hospital with his dad, and he ended up growing up with his dad's parents in the country. The reason I was going through adoption was because I'd found out what kind of people his dad and his dad's family were. All I will say is they were beyond evil and sinister, and if I had to compare them to something, it would be like the movie *The Hills Have Eyes*. This family was bizarre and unbelievable. (You will soon understand what I mean.)

Time went on, and I moved into bigger place because of my sister and my kids, I had just met this yardie, a Jamaican named Ox, and the day I moved into this place I was also washing clothes in the apartment washeteria. I'll never forget this day. Luke and 2 Live Crew were playing at BIG T, and my sister was going. I was home getting my new place together and washing clothes, so I babysat as well. Her ride didn't show up, and while she was looking for her ride, my son's dad popped up (the bizarre one). He had his sister and my son and asked me to keep my son while he took his sister to BIG T. Of course I said yes, and my sister asked if she could ride with them and he said yes.

An hour after they left, I saw the news saying they canceled the show at BIG T because it was a shootout. So I was expecting them to come back soon. It had to be about 3:00 p.m. I remember falling asleep on couch and when I woke up it was dark and late, so I went to get the last round of clothes out of the washeteria. As I walked around the corner, I saw my son's dad's car and it looked like another person was sitting in the front with him. I will spare you the ugly details, but I walked up to window and saw my sister and him together. I was frozen, and when I was able to snap out of it, I walked off in silence toward the washeteria to get my clothes. Then I walked back toward them and toward my apartment. Once I walked in my door, I walked faster toward my bedroom to get my gun on top of my closet. I had every intention of shooting both of them. But my boyfriend at that time (Jamaican Ox) had taken it, so I angrily went to the kitchen to find a knife. I looked up, and those two idiots had followed me to my apartment. They were steady saying, "We wasn't doing nothing, what's wrong with you?" All I remember was throwing what I had in my hand at them and making a phone call. He knew what time it was; I told him I was going to call state troopers and give them his info so they could bust him (because he had drugs in his car going back to his town). He jumped in his car, drove off, and left Tonya at my home.

A few days went by, and yes, my sister was still living with me. Then my friends who was classmates and just so happened to be my male homeboys were there at my home and knew what had happened. I flipped out because Tonya boldly said, "We are gonna be together and not gonna stop seeing each other." She had my nephew in her hands when she said it. I took him out of her hands and began to beat her up till I got tired. My friends knew not to break it up because of the situation. She finally got up and ran out the door to a neighbor's house to use a phone to call the police on me. This would be the first time I ever went to jail. The police who came out just so happened to be two female officers. When they heard what happened and why I beat her up, they literally didn't want to take me jail. They were trying to find some reason to take her as well. But they couldn't because she'd made the phone call to the police. So off to jail I went. I told her to be out of my house before I got out on bond.

Months went by, and the effects of my sister sleeping with my son's dad started to take a toll on me mentally. I was dreaming and constantly thinking of ways to kill both of them. By this time, my son's dad had put my sister into an apartment so they could continue their rendezvouses. I started drinking and plotting how I was going to kill both; I don't think I ever cared about getting away with it. By this time, my entire family knew about this, and as sad as I am to say this, half of them were ok with this behavior and sickness. I can remember my mom telling me, "Well, it's not like it was your husband." Yes, you heard me. I remember feeling like I'd felt when I caught them together: like someone had stuck a knife in my chest. I only had my cousin Jackie—who was like my oldest sister—to cry to.

As time went by, I was not well. It was getting close to Christmas, and my cousin Jackie had picked me and the kids up to go shopping. She said she had to make a stop, but she didn't tell me where. Then we pulled up to my sister's apartment. Then I knew we were stopping at her place. Jackie is and always tried to be the peacemaker, no matter what. As I sat in the car, my cousin got out and went to her apartment door. I was angry and wondering why would she bring me here, knowing I was a ticking time bomb. Nevertheless, I sat and waited for her to come back to the car, and she wasn't alone; my sister and my baby nephew were behind her. I thought it was set up. They got in the car with us and we drove off in silence. I was burning up mad, and my cousin said, "I know you're mad, but she was in that apartment with no lights on and no money." My so-called baby daddy had left her and moved on to the next victim. My nephew, as I said earlier, is my heart like my own son. and so I said nothing.

As we drove, there was a smell in the car that caused us to ride with the windows down; it was like a dead smell. We asked my sister why was she smelling like that, and she said she didn't know and that she had been showering. We came to find out that she had gotten pregnant by this dude and the baby had died in her. So she ended up in the hospital. I remember having all kinds of wicked thoughts and thinking "I can't let this go." I cried and told God, "Thank you for her baby not living, because I would be in prison for rest of my life." Because there was no way I was going to be part of sick freak show with our babies being siblings and cousins at the same time. I literally would have killed her and that child at that time, that's how messed up I felt in this situation. The next thing I knew, I was in my car with a loaded gun and a box of bullets driving ninety miles per hour down I-45 south headed to Ennis to find him. I drove up into the projects and saw his car parked. He was in driver seat, and I saw a young lady in passenger seat. I never saw a baby in the car seat in the back. I literally had out of body experience, I was so full of rage. I walked up to the window and began to shoot into the window at his head. I was an inch away from the door, and all I can say is God was looking out for all of us, because not one bullet hit anyone. He drove off, and I jumped into my car and followed him, shooting at the gas tank; I wanted him dead. We drove through Ennis's dirt roads like a car chase in movie for what seemed like ten minutes before I heard police sirens and I snapped back to reality and turned off and hit the highway back to Dallas in silence. I didn't go straight home because I thought the police would be waiting. I went to my aunt Minnie's apartment, and as soon as I walked in, she said, "Here she is," as she was talking to someone on the phone. She said to me, "You going to jail, you crazy fool. There was a baby in the back seat, and the police said bullets missed the car seat by an inch." I was so full of rage, I told him that if they filed charges, I would kill everybody.

I'm so glad God didn't allow my actions to fall into place and that God looks after fools. Thank God I didn't go jail. I knew I needed help and reached out to a doctor to talk to. Time went on, years went by, and this situation took root in me. I would have flashbacks on my sister at times and spaz out on her, and a few times I would beat her up or tear up her things. It would be many, many years before God delivered me from the hurt, rage, pain, and unforgiveness.

Chapter 9: The Addictions of Crime, Money, and Drugs

Six kids later, my life of crime began. I met my best friend—my sister from another mother—s during the end of that time. Her name is Felica, and by coincidence, her last name is Beasley as well. We ended up committing our first robbery with our male friends, one of whom was a menace and a real killer and jacker. I ended up setting up some young guys in North Dallas, and I can remember telling him, "Do not kill or shoot anyone." As Felica and sat in the car waiting, we watched them draw guns on these poor kids and make them undress and get on the ground. Felica was laughing (she is a person who laughs at everything; we could be in front of firing squad and she would laugh), and I was getting upset because I thought he was going to kill them and we would go to jail. Thank God nobody got hurt. I was shaken up for a while, but it wouldn't be my last time getting us into serious trouble.

I always had something going on. I became a real criminal; I hustled banks, drugs, and I set other drug dealers up. I did everything but sell my body. I was in and out of jail, and God put Mr. Earl Jackson, an attorney, in my life after I caught my first felony case. He went on to become more than just my attorney. I remember calling him collect at his office what seemed like every nine months with a new charge or charges. As the years went by, I was in jail so much that I ended up with five felony probations. Each year, I would violate one with a new charge. That fifth probation, I was looking at thirty years, and God gave me a miracle once again. God sent word saying I wouldn't go prison that time, but to go and sin no more. Well, I was foolish, because I got out and continued criminal activities. I thought I was having the best times of my life because I had money and there was nothing I felt I couldn't do.

As I began to indulge in drugs, I tried premos, cocaine, and pills. I fell in (what I thought was) love with cocaine first. I remember going to one of Dallas's biggest drug dealers' party spots; not anyone could just come. I saw the who's who there, and that's when I saw and thought the cool and heavy dealers did cocaine. But that would change when ecstasy hit the streets and I took my very first Blue Dolphin. Then I thought I was in love with the word ecstasy. I remember taking them every day for a year. I didn't know they put holes in your brain and make you forgetful. I remember spending so much money on those two drugs, I could have bought two homes. I usually always kept cocaine to sell because I had the biggest connections, so I never made and kept the money I should have had. I remember having a connection to this known cartel in East Dallas. And one of my Jamaican friends didn't have any connections, so he would give me $32,000 every two weeks to go get two kilos for him. I remember every time I would go to my cartel connection to get the drugs, they would have one of their relatives sit in one of the cars on the side of their house and count my money.

Then I was given the drugs. The devil had me so fearless and dumb that as this person would be counting stacks, I would also be counting, and out of every stack I counted, I would peel a one hundred dollar bill off and hide it in my shoe. I can only imagine now what they would have done to me if I was caught. But I had already made up my mind that the next round would be the last. I kept telling him he had to pay me more because of the risk I was taking. He kept ignoring me, so I ended taking the last two from him. God was yet covering me. My life of crime was so long and was full of unbelievable situations that I'd need to write a second book just to describe them all.

Chapter 10: Prison Time

I woke up one morning after thinking I was getting ready to go on the run and found out there were eight warrants out for my arrest, including state and one federal warrant. They had what seemed like every law enforcement agency in the U.S. there. I assume this was because of my history of not going quietly, and in past warrant service attempts, they'd had to kick in the door. I don't know. But they came like I was Griselda Blanco. FBI agent Gary Ebbings sat on one side of me and said, "You've been busy, young lady." I had warrants all over Dallas. To be honest, I was tired. I was ready to go lay down and get this over with. Altogether, I was given six years. After I got out, I came home and I tried to work. I actually worked for some top corporations, and I enjoyed working. I got hired at Ernst & Young accounting firm, Acutel, and Fijisti . Each one of those companies let me go because of my background. After getting let go, my spirit was broken, and I went back to what I knew. I started trafficking, and then I hooked up with one of my exes.

He had been a football player and was the branch manager of a bank. We started making money by taking money out of wealthy people's money market accounts. I was making $16,000 a day for two months. and I bought cars and blew the rest. I ended up getting caught with my best friend with forty pounds of weed on our way to Jackson, Mississippi. I got caught in Monroe, Louisiana. Our bonds were both set at $60,000. My people sent the money to my sister to come bond us out. That was another story.

I stayed out on bond for a year before Texas found out I was out on bond (I was still on parole in Texas). My parole office was very cool with me; he let me know ahead of time not to come in. I had blue warrant. I stayed out for additional year. I hired an attorney in Louisiana to deal with that case and was caught and was sent back to prison, and Texas and Louisiana ran the charges together. I did another two years and then came home in 2005; that was it for me. I will say, I tried to do what I called little nonrisky crimes by hooking people up with my connections. So I would make money that way. I enrolled at Richland College. I didn't finish, but I went to work and started working in tax office, and my life took another turn. I was finally done with world of crime and anyone who was doing crime. I started realizing how important your background is, and I hate every bad choice I made.

Chapter 11: Confronting Childhood Trauma

While I was in prison, I wrote and told my mom about the abuse and the horrible things her ex-husband had done. And like many other mothers and relatives, she pretty much said I was lying. I remember being *so* mad and hurt. I wrote back and told her that if she was as close to God as she said, she should ask Him and then ask her ex-husband. She found out I wasn't lying, but I never got an apology.

After I came home from prison, I told her about the sexual abuse I'd endured as a kid. In very confrontational tone, she responded, "Yolanda, when did these things happen, and why you didn't say nothing?" I found out later that my mom had shared with other family members that I was fast. *Wow.*

Chapter 12: God's Drawing Power

I remember going to church one Sunday at Full Gospel Holy Temple. I was still in the world, going to clubs, dating many people, and going from one failed relationship to the next. I had no interest of coming back to the Lord; I had been back-sliding and had not been in the will of God for years. I just wanted to go to church for some reason. I kept going off and on for years, but I was never ready to surrender.

I ended up going into business with my first cousin who was closer to me than my sister; I would do anything for her. It went very bad—so bad I almost let the devil trick me off the streets, possibly for rest my life. I won't get into detail, but the situation had me so stressed out that I began experiencing symptoms of an undiagnosed diseased I didn't know I had. I could hardly complete sentences, my head was hurting, I had pain in my hands, back, and legs, and a lot more. I stood up one day and fell to the ground.

I was admitted to the hospital and diagnosed with Chiari malformation type 1, a genetic disease. I was in the hospital for almost two weeks and from there I went to a nursing home. As I lay in the hospital, I remember telling God I didn't want to surrender because of my situation—imagine that! I'm grateful God didn't turn me over to myself and thoughts. All I remember is in that bed I totally surrendered to the Lord. And that night my life changed for good. I began to seek God and, really for the first time, know what it is to hunger after Christ and His will and Word. I was still struggling with what happened with the business situation in my heart, and God sent me same word three times: He told me not to retaliate and to forgive, and if I obeyed, not only was He gonna prepare a table in the presence of my enemies, but he was gonna bless my business beyond what I could imagine. And I tell you, He did just that.

God blew my mind, not just getting my business off the ground but blessing it. Remember, my attorney who was representing me in my criminal charges? Well, he believed in me when my own mom didn't, and he gave me the money to start my business. I went home and cried and began to worship God for doing what He said He would do. But my greatest trials would soon start.

My health would only get worse, and the spiritual warfare was on. I truly found out that *health is wealth*. It seemed the closer I got to Christ, the worse my health got. I was then diagnosed with congestive heart failure after almost dying. I woke up one morning and it looked like someone put a fat suit on me. I had twelve hospital stays in one year, and still God allowed me to run my business from a hospital bed. The business continued to grow, but the attacks on my health got worse. The next year, I was laying in my bed for over month feeling depressed, and I didn't know why. I literally went blind in one eye and was peeing every five minutes. The Spirit prompted me to get in my car to drive to the hospital. A truck ended up hitting me, and an ambulance came and rushed me to hospital. When I got there, they asked me if anyone had told me I was a diabetic. I said, "No, why?"

The doctor said, "Your sugar is 784."

God once again blew my mind, and I was diagnosed with diabetes. God's deliverance was evident in my life and in that situation. There would be many other near-death experiences, *but God.* I didn't know I had blood clots in both lungs and was laying with my new grandson and couldn't breathe. I got to the hospital in time again. In the midst of these attacks on my health, God yet showed Himself mighty and faithful. I was laying up and recovering when God gave me the vision for my nonprofit: Redeeming Women Walking in Excellence. This organization will draw women to Christ and provide temporary shelter for women with tough backgrounds or those who are getting out of jail or prison. The doors have not opened yet due to the fight with my health. But I tell you, God's word is forever settled and He is faithful. He is. I tell you, every time the enemy attacks me, God turns it for His good to show me and others He is God.

I went in for gastric bypass surgery in April. The doctor hit a main artery, and I began to bleed out. I wasn't supposed to make it. They had to abort the surgery and get me upstairs to emergency surgery to stop the bleeding. I now have a huge hematoma in my belly that has to take a year to shrink. And I'm still having complications. But to God be glory, I'm still here, and God is still keeping me alive.

I didn't share most of the ugly, worldly episodes from my life in this book because I wanted God to get the glory first and foremost. I want to say to anyone who has had childhood trauma, a parent or parents who didn't show you love or treated you differently than your siblings, to anyone who has felt like a black sheep or has been told you would never be anything or amount to anything, I promise you God is faithful. God will be more to you than you ever thought you needed—more to you than your mama, your daddy, and everyone else.

I pray that this book encourages just one person, and I dare you to try God no matter what situation you're in. God loves you and will send or replace others in your life that you're not genetically tied to who will pour into you and believe in you.

Last, I pray for and encourage every young lady who is pregnant at a young age, who encounters molestation, or who didn't have a parent to believe in them.

John 3:16 says, "For God so loved the world, that he gave his only begotten Son, that whosoever believeth in him should not perish, but have everlasting life" (KJV).

Romans 8:18 says, "For I reckon that the sufferings of this present time are not worthy to be compared with the glory which shall be revealed in us" (KJV).

I'd like to thank God who is truly my strong tower, my love, and my everything.

I have to thank my dad, James David Carter, for the impact he had in my life for the time he was here in land of living. The love I felt as child was so explosive; I'm grateful to have experienced such love from him.

I'd like to thank my mom for being there for my kids when I was in and out of jail.

I have to thank Mr. Earl Jackson and the whole Jackson firm for everything—not just for being my attorney, but my friend, too, and for always being brutally honest. And for taking every collect call from jail!

About the Author

Yolanda Beasley was born & raised in Dallas, Tx, and is the oldest of one other sister of her father James Davide Carter and Linda Beasley. She has 6 biological children, all of whom are grown (2 girls & 4 boys), and has 15 grandchildren (3 sets of twins). Yolanda Beasley is a single woman of GOD. She lives her life truly walking in the will of GOD and believing the gospel and return of CHRIST. She attended LAKE HIGHLANDS HIGH SCHOOL IN NORTH DALLAS TX, and also attended RICHLAND JR COLLEGE, where she studied business. Yolanda Beasley is now an entrepreneur and continues writing as an author.

www.ingramcontent.com/pod-product-compliance
Lightning Source LLC
Chambersburg PA
CBHW051937150726
47999CB00006B/2261